alo: the bosom, the center
ha: the breath of life
Aloha is a *feeling*. It's not just a word or a greeting.
You're conveying or bestowing the feeling. You share
this with people when you greet them.
— **Hannah Veary**

The 'aloha spirit' — however it is defined — is a basic
ingredient of a style of life based on the essential
equality and dignity of all human beings. The basic
qualities of this way of life are perhaps best
characterized by openness, hospitality, neighborly
concern, tolerance, genuine love for other
people...Hawaii as an image and as a state of mind is
heavily indebted to the original Hawaiians.
— from *Hawaii 2000,* **George Chaplin**
and **Glenn D. Paige,** editors, © 1973,
The University of Hawaii Press.

Hawaii
Times Editions
422 Thomson Road, Singapore 1129.

© Copyright by Times Editions, 1986.
Typeset by Superskill, Singapore.
Colour separation by Colourscan, Singapore.
Printed by Tien Wah Press, Singapore.

ISBN: 9971-40-010-3

HAWAII

Photography by Frank Salmoiraghi
Text by Jocelyn Fujii
Edited and Designed by Leonard Lueras

LES·EDITIONS·DU·PACIFIQUE

Contents

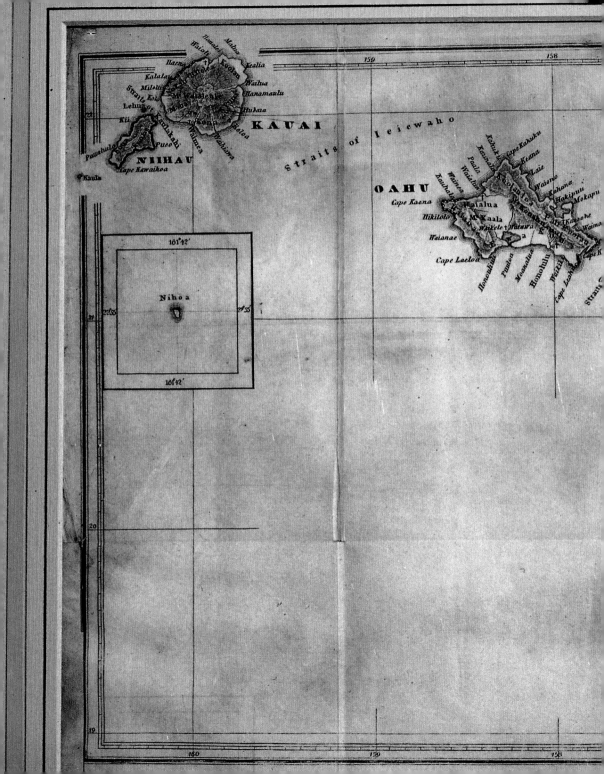

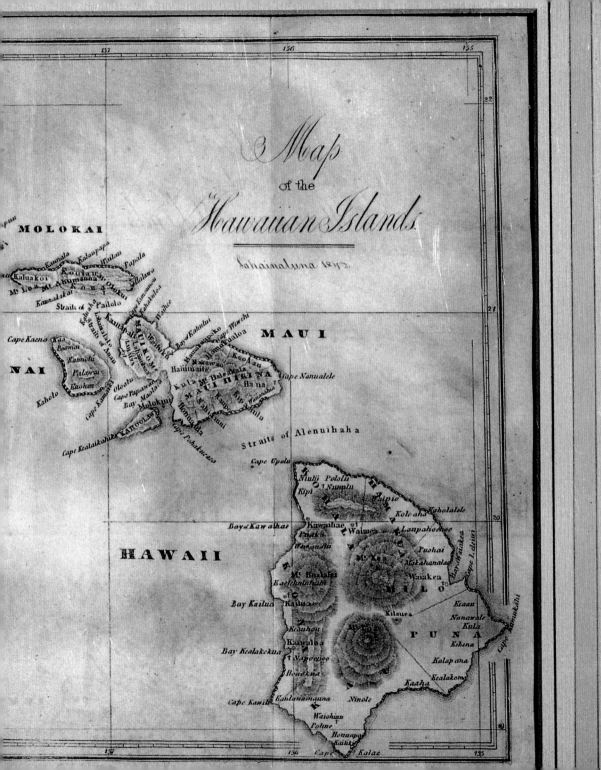

Map

of the

Hawaiian Islands

Lahainaluna 1843.

MOLOKAI

MAUI

NAI

HAWAII

Straits of Alenuihaha

PUNA

HILO

The Place

Hawaii's story is the story of creation, of great volumes of molten earth surging through the elements to form peaks that will touch snow, valleys that house gods, and shorelines, jagged or inviting, where lava once singed — or still singes — the sea.

This story spans grand summits and great depths. It begins 3,000 feet underwater, where the summit of an active volcano is inching its way upward. Loihi, as this seamount is called, is the embryo of what will be the newest island in the Hawaiian chain, an archipelago said to have formed some two to twenty-five million years ago as similar volcanoes surfaced, rose and then towered as islands.

About 30 miles southwest of the active volcano Kilauea on the Big Island of Hawaii, Loihi is forming inch by inch over a hot volcanic vent most recently vacated by the southernmost island, Hawaii. She is emerging through a process called tectonic plate movement. As the Hawaiian Islands ride passively atop a slowly moving plate on the earth's surface, the heat of the stationary vent is feeding the formation of this newest infant in a geological laboratory called the Hawaiian Islands. Scientists say it may be 10,000 years before she is a bona fide island. But rather than hold their breath or merely envision her development, geologists and marine researchers are studying Loihi for her minerals and geological features — information that sheds light on the creative processes of Hawaii itself.

Stretching toward the northwest from this new islet in the sea are the youngest Hawaiian island, the Big Island of Hawaii, and then Maui, Kahoolawe, Lanai, Molokai, Oahu, Kauai and privately owned Niihau with its small population of Hawaiians. All but Kahoolawe are populated pockets of paradise in an archipelago that actually continues far north, into a little-known part of Hawaii called the Northwestern Hawaiian Islands. Indeed, few people know that the State of Hawaii consists of the eight major islands plus 124 minor islands. Nearly 2,400 miles away from the nearest continent, the Hawaiian Islands stand splendid-

Facing page: The feisty Kilauea Volcano on the Big Island sends forth yet another fiery emission in April, 1985. Above: Waxy, stark anthuriums, such as this one from Puna on the Big Island, make up a good portion of Hawaii's $36-million-a-year flower and nursery product industry.

ly in the Pacific, removed from all else but one another.

With their collective land mass of 4.1 million acres or 6,450 square miles, these islands form the fourth smallest state in the U.S. They also embrace an imposing physical landscape that ranges from saw-toothed cliffs to desolate, moon-like craters and peaks that rise nearly 14,000 feet into the clouds.

Scattered across Hawaii's green-carpeted craters, dense tropical valleys, ranch lands, shorelines and thickly populated high-rise jungles are a resident population of 1,039,000. Nearly 30 percent of the islanders are of mixed race, the polyglot makings of a magnificent indigenous people that mingled freely with waves of immigrants who came to these shores. And the population today is relatively young, with a median age of slightly over 28 years. With a daily influx of visitors, a high percentage of military residents and new immigrant arrivals that pour in still from Southeast Asian shores, Hawaii's complexion is becoming in-

Facing page: Hawaii is for skiers too, who find in the snow-lined summit of Mauna Kea a blinding, transcendent beauty. Below: A changing portrait of turquoise occurs daily at Nanakuli on Oahu's leeward coastline, not far from the famous Makaha Beach surfing spot.

creasingly multi-ethnic in its character.

In 1957, this ethnographic evolution prompted novelist May Sarton to write:

"These islands, as they slowly greened over, had attracted human migrants in waves, first the Polynesians bringing taro, dogs, bananas in their canoes and setting up the primitive principalities and powers of what eventually became Hawaiian royalty; the whalers, the sandalwood merchants, the missionaries, the sugar planters and ranchers, the Chinese and Japanese traders and laborers, and finally the tourists. We were among the last to come...But on this evening we felt the enchantment and the peril of living on the island volcano, born in fire, flowering, and slowly dying in an illimitable relentless blue of sea and sky."

As of 1984, this chop-suey society included some 180,000 Japanese, 45,000 Chinese, 17,000 Portuguese and numerous Samoans, Koreans, Filipinos, Vietnamese and miscellaneous others.

Facing page: Celebrations honoring Hawaii's Prince Jonah Kuhio usually occur in March. At Honolulu's Prince Kuhio School, the ti-leaf and flower-bedecked tribute attracts even the diaper set. Below: Ladies of the Kaahumanu Society dress somberly for their treks to the Royal Mausoleum in Nuuanu, where Hawaii's Kamehameha kings and queens rest.

14

A Pacific Magnet

Even before the first Polynesian voyagers arrived in Hawaii, sometime between 500 and 800 A.D., these islands were a glistening magnet in the Pacific — first for hardy migratory birds such as the *kolea*, or golden plover, and then for settlers who followed in their hand-hewn canoes. Fixing their sights on the stars and navigating with a sophisticated and intuitive knowledge of wind, cloud and ocean patterns, these remarkable Polynesians from the Marquesas Islands boldly sailed northward and are believed to have been the first humans to make the difficult 2,000-mile ocean-crossing to Hawaii. They also sailed east to Easter Island and southwest to New Zealand.

It was centuries after the Marquesans' landfall in Hawaii — in about 1200 A.D. — that a second wave of South Seas settlers arrived, also from Eastern Polynesia. They came from Tahiti, the Society Islands, and they named their new home Hawai'i. In race, history, physical features, traditions, language, religion and the arts, the people known as the Hawaiians bear unmistakable similarities to the Tahitians.

This link between Hawaii and her Polynesian relatives will continue to inspire and fascinate, even as it did in Captain James Cook's time. After landing in Hawaii in 1778, Cook marveled at the similarities of language in Hawaii, New Zealand and Tahiti, a kinship that prompted him to call Polynesia "the most extensive nation on earth."

Besides bringing their language, the first Polynesian voyagers also brought plants and animals integral to their survival. They filled their sturdy canoes with pigs and dogs and, according to the *Atlas of Hawaii*, they brought 25 species of plants used for "food, fiber, shelter, and medicine." Among the plants were *kukui*, used as candlenuts, breadfruit, taro, coconut, *wauke* (from which they made *kapa*, or bark cloth), yams, sugar cane and *ti*. All but *wauke* are in abundant use today, including the Hawaiians' staple, taro, described by the writer Mark Twain as a "corpulent sweet potato".

Introduced botanical species wrought ecological

Preceding pages: *A ghostly beauty is created by the surf pounding on the jagged coastline of Hana in East Maui.* **Facing page:** *The wooden figure of Ku, the Hawaiian god of war, appears at the Pu'uhonua O Honaunau National Historical Park, also called the City of Refuge, on the Big Island.* **Above:** *Lono, the god of thunder, is also represented at the City of Refuge.*

changes in an environment that supported about 2,200 endemic plants that grew only in Hawaii. A recent survey showed that more than 1,100 species, sub-species and varieties of native flora are either endangered and threatened or extinct. Plants such as *ohia*, the first to sprout from a lava flow, *koa* (used in furniture and old surfboards) and several types of ferns found deep in the mountains are among the more common endemic plants that have survived.

Today Hawaii is known for its parade of fresh fruits that mark the seasons: papayas, mangoes, pineapple, lichee, mountain apples, bananas, coconuts, any one of which — except for the rare mountain apple and lichee — you may find adorning your poolside tropical drink. And at *hula* festivals or performances, the *haku* (woven or plaited) head or neck *lei* worn by the dancers will contain endemic and indigenous plants, the chief ingredients in *hula* costuming.

Notes the *Atlas of Hawaii*: "The isolation of the

Hawaiian Island chain from other land masses, the isolation between the separate islands in the chain, the equable but variable climate, the topography which leads to the isolation of small populations in deep valleys or separate mountain peaks, and isolation brought by lava flows...are all factors which have permitted evolution to occur at an especially rapid rate."

That evolution also has affected the fauna of Hawaii, which includes many rare birds that live nowhere else but in the dense uplands of the less populated Neighbor Islands. Creatures such as the Hawaiian goose, called the *nene*, for example, like living on desolate lava flows and at high elevations such as Maui's Haleakala Crater and Mauna Loa on the Big Island. Some species of colorful honeycreepers, such as the *'i'iwi* and the vermilion *'apapane*, have evolved into multiple varieties from a single species that arrived eons ago. They are the survivors — but barely — among a fragile

Facing page: Hawaiian temples, or heiau, *were built of stone, such as this one (above) at the Pu'ukohola Heiau National Historical Site on the Big Island. Below, Molokai's famous phallic rock is said to have potent fertility-evoking powers. Below: Hawaii's rare* nene *geese are captured in the eerie silence of Maui's Haleakala, where they live amid the silverswords and other rare flora.*

17

18

lot: about two-fifths of the 67 different varieties of Hawaiian birds found in the 19th-century are now thought to be extinct, while many others are considered endangered or rare.

Like plants such as the *ohelo*, *mamane* and silversword, these Hawaiian birds maintain a fragile existence in the wilderness areas that are also the most awesome physical presences in Hawaii. Thus, a hardy backpacker traversing Maui's 10,000-foot Mount Haleakala will often see rare *nene* waddling among spectacular silverswords that are dazzling in their silvery, mandala-like forms. On the 13,796-foot-high Mauna Kea on the Big Island, dark-rumped petrels nest and the native *elepaio* bird sings out through dry *mamane* forests. And only in the depths of the Alakai Swamp, atop Kauai's Mount Waialeale, the wettest spot on earth, will you see a mysterious and elusive little bird called the *o'o*. Listen closely and you may be one of the lucky few who hear the plaintive call of this soulful little survivor.

Preceding pages: *The purple vanda, top left, the yellow protea, top right, the lotus, below it, and the torch-like pink protea are in rainbowed contrast to the taro leaf, shown close-up in its glorious symmetry.* **Facing page:** *A Kailua-Kona sunset, above, and a misty North Kohala scene on the Big Island give a glimpse of the island's offerings.* **Below:** *the 300-foot Hiilawe twin falls in the Big Island's Waipio Valley.*

Historical Notes

In the days before Western contact, the ancient Hawaiians lived in a society that had no money, no concept of private land ownership and aesthetic and practical values that placed bird feathers and *kapa* among their most valuable possessions. There were the *ali'i* — the royalty — and the *makaainana* — commoners — and in between a class of priests and seers called *kahuna*, who guided the culture in everything from crafts to medicine and navigation.

The Hawaiian spiritual pantheon, inherited from their Polynesian ancestors, emphasized four major gods and a host of lesser deities. The primary god was Kane, the god of sunlight and nature; Kanaloa, the lord of the sea; Ku, the god of war; and Lono, the god of thunder. Other important deities were Pele, the volcano goddess and goddess of fire, and Laka, the patron goddess of the *hula* to which all dance performances were traditionally dedicated.

It was during a festival honoring the god Lono that the English explorer Captain James Cook — who was mistaken for a white Lono — first arrived in Hawaii with his cache of firearms, nails and iron implements, and flora and fauna from the West — thereby opening what became known as Hawaii's post-contact period. In February, 1778, during his third major Pacific voyage, Cook sailed into Waimea, Kauai, with his ships, *HMS Resolution* and *HMS Discovery*. The sight of these masted ships off Waimea caused quite a stir, prompting some Hawaiians to wonder if they were floating islands or "trees moving on the sea." Cook and his men departed from that sojourn rejuvenated and laden with bartered yams and other supplies.

The following year, Cook landed at the Big Island's Kealakekua Bay, and after a skirmish over a stolen cutter was killed with some of his men. Thus, on February 14, 1779, Cook's brief period of glory in the landfall he named the Sandwich Islands came to an abrupt and violent end.

The Hawaiians, meanwhile, had inherited from their visitors major venereal and common (but previously unknown in Hawaii) diseases and firearms to fuel their

Preceding pages: *An 18th Century print depicts the baptism of a Hawaiian chief aboard a French ship.* Facing page: *Elaborate tattoos and hair bleached with lime from coral characterized ancient Hawaiian women.* Above: *Captain James Cook, who discovered Hawaii in 1778.*

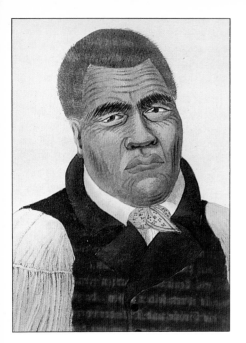

Facing page: *These French studies of Hawaiian women and men reveal their artistry in self-adornment and a strong Western influence.*
Above: *Kamehameha the Great, who unified the Hawaiian Islands.*

wars. Both elements accounted for a significant decline in the Hawaiian population: In less than a century after "contact" with the West, the Hawaiian population, estimated to be about 300,000, shrank to about 60,000.

Some historians also claim that the introduction of firearms by Westerners hastened the unification of the Islands under one ruler. It was in 1795, after Kamehameha the Great won a final and decisive Battle of Nuuanu on the island of Oahu, that six of the eight populated Hawaiian Islands first came under one chief's rule. The last two islands, Kauai and Niihau, joined by tacit agreement 15 years later.

Kamehameha's death in 1819 ushered into power his son Liholiho, who became Kamehameha II, and two widows, all of whom are remembered for abolishing an ancient *kapu* (taboo) system that had for many centuries imposed severe restrictions on women, commoners and others, depending on their caste and rank.

In the next seven and a half decades, six more Hawaiian monarchs ruled these Islands as they became increasingly open to European, American and, later, Asian influences. As industries such as whaling and the arrival of Christian missionaries (in 1820) soon established Hawaii as an international gateway, ancient Hawaiian customs, religion and arts declined.

Meanwhile, following the introduction of laws regarding private land ownership, beginning with the *Great Mahele* (or land division) in the 1840s, sugar became established as a major industry and the ethnic influx began. Chinese, Japanese, Portuguese, Filipinos and other ethnic groups poured into Hawaii as contract laborers for sugar plantations. King David Kalakaua, who opened the way for contract labor from Japan, ruled a kingdom divided along racial lines — whites against the minorities — until stripped of his power by a ruling white minority in 1887. His successor, Queen Liliuokalani, the composer of *Aloha ʻOe*, was abruptly deposed in 1893 by American revolutionaries in what was acknowledged to be an illegal overthrow but a very successful *coup d'etat*. Hawaii's monarchy thus came to an ignoble end and Hawaii became a territory in 1900. Bolstered by proof of its loyalty following the 1941 bombing of Pearl Harbor, Hawaii eased happily into official American statehood in 1959.

27

Oahu-Honolulu

On a certain bright morning the Islands hove in sight, lying low on the lonely sea...As we approached, the imposing promontory of Diamond Head rose up out of the ocean, its rugged front softened by the hazy distance, and presently the details of the land began to make themselves manifest: first the line of beach; then the plumed cocoanut trees of the tropics; then cabins of the natives; then the white town of Honolulu...
— from *Mark Twain in Hawaii*, 1866

Honolulu has changed dramatically since Mark Twain's first beatific glimpse in 1866. The "line of beach" is still there as Waikiki, but now it's studded with hotels, oil-drenched bodies and a potpourri of beachside businesses purveying everything from passion fruit smoothies to windsurfing lessons. Diamond Head, meanwhile, still holds vigil as it always has, like a detached and queenly goddess, over Oahu, the third largest of the Hawaiian Islands.

As your plane makes its landing approach, Diamond Head will be visible at the southern end of the string of glimmering high-rises that are unmistakably Waikiki. The fingers of water on the other side of your aerial field of vision are parts of sprawling Pearl Harbor, and straight ahead is a range of Oahu's central mountains, called the Koolaus, separated by a plain from its western counterpart, the Waianae mountain range. Out of view, on the other side of the Koolau range, is windward Oahu, dominated by vast spreads of suburban residences and military facilities curled around long stretches of white sand beaches. The Waianae mountains define the dry leeward coast on western Oahu, and the North Shore stands alone as the surfing hotspot of Hawaii and the world. The south shore of Oahu embraces downtown Honolulu, Waikiki and board and bodysurfing swells that are anathema for beginners but tube-riding heaven for the pros.

This, sprawled beneath your descending plane, is Honolulu: Honolulu Harbor, where a major maritime

Preceding pages: *An unusual view of Diamond Head is captured from lower Manoa Valley.* **Facing page:** *Beyond Waikiki's famous "Wall" is a favorite local boogie boarding spot where surfers enjoy smooth rides facing Waikiki's dense skyline of high-rise hotels.* **Above:** *A ubiquitous sight in Hawaii — flower leis.*

revitalization is being planned; downtown, with its mirrored high-rise buildings; residences creeping up hillsides like brush fires; parks, hotels and beaches peppered with sun-worshipping bodies; and yes, surfers and *hula* girls, the stuff of every visitor's dreams. This is Honolulu, capital of the state of Hawaii and a county encompassing the entire island, where close to 80 percent of the state's population lives and where life moves faster than on any of the other islands.

The Hawaii Visitors Bureau estimates that more than 67,000 visitors are on this 608-square-mile island on any given day. If you're one of them, you'll arrive at the Honolulu International Airport, where amid the noise, crowds and smell of jet exhaust you may catch the welcome whiff of *plumeria* (frangipani) or some equally exotic scent. Look around. You'll see flower *leis* around people's necks or dangling from the bronzed arms of lovely Polynesian greeters representing various tour companies. Whether or not the *lei* is

The campy ladies of today's Kodak Hula Show depict a style and image of Hawaii that could have come straight from a Hawaii picture book of the '40s. Below them is Hawaii's bastion of tourism, Waikiki, shown in a **mauka** *view from Manoa Valley.*

for you, inhale deeply and enjoy, for the drive from the airport to Waikiki is an industrial purgatory.

And if the taxi or bus driver sounds like he's speaking Swahili, it may be pidgin English, a plantation patois prevailing in local parlance, or the unorthodox — but highly efficient — geographical directions used on Oahu. "How you figgah?" *Ewa* (EH-vah) means west; Diamond Head, east; *mauka* (MAU-kuh), toward the mountains; and *makai* (mah-KYE), toward the sea. Once you've mastered these terms, you can feel that much less a *malihini* — newcomer — in this island place called Hawaii.

Wicky-Wacky Waikiki

So you've survived the drive through Honolulu's factory-ridden, smoke-choked airport corridor and you've arrived in Waikiki, the Disneyland of beach vacation fantasies. This mile-and-a-half long strip of

Facing page: A Japanese tourist literally flips over Waikiki Beach while other tourists gather for their smorgasbord of water sports in front of the Royal Hawaiian Hotel. Below: A few feet from a lagoon where gregarious porpoises hold court, the Kahala Hilton's pool attracts its share of bathers even though the beach is a few feet away.

coastline is really a series of about six smaller beaches with names known mainly by locals — such as Gray's Beach, the Royal-Moana Beach and, at the Diamond Head end just beyond Waikiki, the Sans Souci beach which once was extolled by no less a personage than Robert Louis Stevenson.

This magnificent but heavily peopled beach called Waikiki — "Spouting Water" — once bordered a swampy marshland inhabited by ducks and other cavorting creatures and was favored by Hawaiian royalty for its fine fishing and gentle, rideable waves. Today it is the densest concentration of concrete in the Islands, weighted by 34,000 hotel and condominium units and scads of people soaking up the sun over surfboards and rum-rich *mai tais* on what its promoters claim these days is "life's greatest beach."

Beachside entrepreneurs are there to cater to your every need, with surfing lessons, sailboards, snorkeling gear, styrofoam body boards and many a tale of the

halcyon days of Waikiki. Looking out toward the sea, you can see parasails and catamarans dotting the horizon and ubiquitous surfers zipping by on their fiberglass fantasies. Behind you, pedicabs, buses, cars and tourists fill one of the city's busiest thoroughfares, Kalakaua Avenue.

There is, too, a good measure of streetside kitsch competing with the sun-drenched allure of the beach. Vendors along the main stretch hawk mounds of electronic gear, souvenirs and trinkets, t-shirts and "crafts" made mostly in Taiwan, Korea or the Philippines. Meanwhile, a parade of *muumuus* and matching aloha shirts continues to assault the senses.

Not to worry. If you keep your sense of humor, Waikiki can be great fun. For one thing, it has a corner on the nightlife, and *haute cuisine* is alive and well in some of Waikiki's deluxe hotels. There's also an ample array of ethnic and American foods in a combination of cafes, hideaways, coffee shops and fast food stands.

Even crowded Waikiki has its own charm and quiet moments of beauty. Consider the beginning windsurfer on a glassy lagoon in Waikiki (facing page) and, below him, the surrealistic glow of the Queen's Surf pavilion. The light turns amber on a sunset boat cruise off Waikiki, below.

Parallel to Kalakaua Avenue is Kuhio Avenue, featuring a predominantly gay district on its *ewa* end and a "pink light" district on the Diamond Head side. The *ewa* end of Kuhio remains a bastion of style and a center for some of the island's best informal dining. There are sidewalk eateries, streetside chic, a couple of vintage art deco Waikiki homes and both sublime and zany people-watching.

For daytime outings, neighboring Diamond Head-side attractions include the Waikiki Aquarium, with its illustrious shark tank and world-renowned nautiluses and, across the street, the Honolulu Zoo and Kapiolani Park, the sprawling, 100-acre domain of joggers, picnickers, kite-fliers and outdoor enthusiasts.

Waikiki is merely the best-known of a string of stunning beaches that make up Oahu's south shore. Actually, though, the real south shore begins at Ala Moana Park a few miles *ewa* of Waikiki. It is the favorite park of local folks who gather there for

Facing page: While sunbathers employ all manner of tanning paraphernalia, others take the more active route, such as the surfers (below) at the Buffalo's Long Board Contest at Makaha Beach, Oahu. Below: Hawaii's underwater pleasures are making ocean recreation one of the state's fastest growing industries.

exercise and entertainment. Though the waters off Ala Moana offer abysmal snorkeling, this form of bounty awaits you past Diamond Head and Koko Head at an underwater park and marine sanctuary called Hanauma Bay. Hanauma is noted for its close-up, technicolor snorkeling, fish that will eat out of your hand and the wall-to-wall people who line its crescent beach like a well-oiled carpet.

Around a lava-tiered corner from Hanauma is Sandy Beach, an occasionally treacherous but eminently watchable bodysurfing spot much loved by shapely teenie-boppers and their muscular surfer boyfriends. Bodysurfing here, or at neighboring Makapuu, is not recommended for novices.

"Yeah, the south shore," exudes one inveterate beachgoer. "It's easy to get to, blindingly beautiful, and it keeps you on your toes. At Makapuu you don't know whether to look up at the hang-gliders or down at the surfers." The choice is yours.

The North Shore

About 45 minutes by freeway from downtown Honolulu, Oahu's North Shore is accessible through central Oahu or Kamehameha Highway along the windward coastline. With its world-famous surfing spots — with waves known to reach 35 feet in the winter — the North Shore appeals to everyone, if not for its surfing and snorkeling, then for its idyllic charm and inimitable local flavor. Nature lovers can take to the plants and birds of Waimea Falls Park while sports enthusiasts and shell-pickers congregate at the abundant shoreline. Even aficionados of shave ice, a beloved local specialty, have their day in the sun, for Haleiwa on the North Shore is known for this icy snow cone treat. And the beaches — Waimea Bay, Ke Iki, Ehukai (where bodysurfing championships are held), the Banzai Pipeline and Sunset Beach — and the smaller snorkeling and diving spots of Shark's Cove and

Facing page: The endless pleasures of the wave range from the perils of Waimea Bay, top, to the tube-riding heaven of a surfer at Velzyland, the last in a string of fabled surfing breaks on the North Shore of Oahu. Below: A brave young boogie-boarder takes on the night surf outside Waikiki Beach.

Three Tables — all line the North Shore in one stunning turn after another.

Downtown

Downtown Honolulu is definitely for dallying. Before you attack the menu of downtown attractions, however, two must-see spots in other parts of town are the Bernice Pauahi Bishop Museum and the Honolulu Academy of Arts, a pair of institutions that are among the most renowned cultural resources in the Pacific. While the Bishop Museum houses the state's largest repository of anthropological and historical displays, the Academy of Arts near Thomas Square contains a collection of ancient and modern works with a strong emphasis on the arts of Asia.

Downtown's offerings embrace the powerful presence of Iolani Palace, this country's only palace and the site of Queen Liliuokalani's tragic demise in 1893.

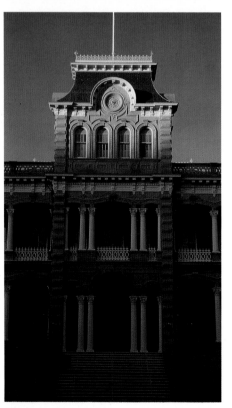

Facing page: *Details of downtown Honolulu include a sun-bathed corner of the Territorial Building, top, the majestic architecture of Iolani Palace, and the Royal Guard at the Royal Mausoleum in Honolulu, bottom.* Above: *Pat Hammond and Patti Chong enjoy their newly refurbished gallery, the Art Loft, in downtown's fast-changing Chinatown while, at left, Chinatown comes alive with its traditional Chinese New Year's lion dance.*

At lunch hour on Fridays, the Royal Hawaiian Band offers free concerts under the large shade trees on the palace grounds, creating an ambience of elegance reminiscent of Hawaii's monarchial period.

About five blocks away is Chinatown, charming with its open-air markets of pungent fresh fish and produce, exotic acupuncture and herbal shops and Chinese restaurants with their own devout followings. Some of Hawaii's most successful artists and painters have opened studios in Chinatown in what may become a revitalization of the area in the arts.

But in Chinatown, it is the weathered, soulful faces of elderly Orientals who tell the real story. They linger on the sidewalks or along the river at the nearby Chinese Cultural Plaza, holding in their presence fading memories of Hawaii's immigrant past. All around them in Chinatown are *lei* shops, beehives of activity where fragrant garlands may be purchased.

Facing page: The Japanese influence in Hawaii is glimpsed through sumo *wrestling, the blessings of a Shinto priest, and* sansei *third-generation Japanese-American artists.* **Below:** *The ineffable splendor of a downtown Honolulu sunset, seen here from the Aloha Tower observation deck.* **Preceding pages:** *Graduates at the University of Hawaii — Manoa .*

Maui

After a quick 25 minutes by plane from Honolulu — or a direct flight from the U.S. mainland on either of two airlines — the island of Maui will come upon you like the seductive scent of gardenia. Empowered with romantic physical attractions and a rarefied grace and beauty, this second largest of the Hawaiian Islands has been known to snare the unsuspecting as a goddess or mistress would.

To begin with, there are upcountry wilderness and crisp mountain air, waterfalls and flower farms, Hawaii's only vineyard and magnificent beaches lining the western coastline. Forty miles of a 150-mile tidal shoreline is developed, and less than five percent of its 729-square-mile terrain is actually inhabited.

Maui is also distinctively chic, with a casual sophistication all its own. And it is a busy little county, for Maui County includes not only the island of Maui, but also Molokai, Lanai and an uninhabited, 45-square-mile island called Kahoolawe (which in recent years has been used as a military island).

Maui is dubbed the Valley Island for the myriad valleys, waterfalls and topographic dimples that course through her terrain. Geographically, Maui consists of East and West Maui, connected by an isthmus, and upcountry Maui, encompassing the dome and slopes of the 10,023-foot-high Haleakala, or House of the Sun, a 19-square-mile volcanic crater that last erupted in 1790.

Legend has it that the demigod Maui restored balance to day and night when he crept up to the edge of Haleakala Crater and ambushed the sun at dawn. The island had only a few short hours of daylight because of the sun's penchant for sleeping long hours and then scampering quickly across the sky. Maui, annoyed to no end over this very *manini* (small) handout of light, lassoed the sun's rays and prepared to demolish it. However, legend holds that Maui succeeded in his mission when the sun promised to slow its pace across the sky and allow longer days to smile upon the island. Today Haleakala is still one of the world's finest natural balconies for viewing and experiencing the mystical power of a sunrise.

Preceding pages: *Sailboats dotting Lahaina Harbor in West Maui.* Facing page: *The mysterious mound is Alau Island, a seabird sanctuary off East Maui's Hana coast.* Above: *This similarly sky-reaching promontory is the famous sculptured peak of Maui's Iao Valley, Iao Needle.*

With Head in the Clouds

Haleakala is a federal park that boasts 27,350 acres, nearly a million visitors a year, and three cabins for overnight guests (interspersed throughout the floor of the crater). As the highest elevation on the island, Haleakala is also the major geographical presence on Maui and a purveyor of many awesome miles of wilderness hiking in the crater — along the Kaupo Gap on the crater's southern flank, and along the Polipoli Loop Trail on the southwestern flank of the mountain. Towns such as Kula, Pukalani and Makawao, with their distinctively *paniolo* (cowboy) flavor, are considered "upcountry" Maui. The term itself evokes images of eucalyptus forests and jacaranda trees, breathtaking panoramas of the West Maui mountains and rich volcanic soil that yields some of the most beautiful flowers in the world. Agricultural Maui specialties generally come from upcountry: Kula onions, protea

blossoms and "Maui Wowee," a world-famous hybrid of a weed known as *pakalolo*. *Pakalolo*, or marijuana, is considered by many to be Hawaii's number one cash crop industry, and the plant is known to thrive happily on Haleakala's volcanic soil.

On the southwestern slopes of Haleakala, where sheep and cattle graze contentedly on Ulupalakua Ranch lands, the Tedeschi Vineyard, Hawaii's only wine-producing place, continues to produce its Blanc de Noirs champagne, another pride of Maui.

Some of the island's most dazzling scenery unfolds beneath the highway as you drive past the Tedeschi Vineyard. Comfortably adrift from the beaten path, this country road overlooks Molokini Islet, a crescent-shaped marine preserve, and ancient lava flows carpeted in green and rolling toward the lava-fringed sea. It is in places like this where you begin to understand why the author Mark Twain called Hawaii "the loveliest fleet of islands anchored in any sea."

Facing page: *"Upcountry" Maui means the silverswords of Haleakala Crater and one of the magical views from Haleakala, of Maalaea Bay and the West Maui mountains.* **Below:** *A Haleakala landscape in all its primordial and pristine splendor.*

Go West, Young Man

Except for the few hardy souls committed to staying in the virginal hinterlands of East or upcountry Maui, the vast majority of the island's two million visitors plop their luggage, dollars and hope into West Maui locations. That's fine with the folks on Maui, who intended from the beginning to confine tourist development to the western shoreline. In spite of its teeming resorts, the island has managed to retain a healthy balance between points of activity and planes of oblivious retreat.

West Maui resorts include Kaanapali, Kapalua, Napili, Wailea, Kihei and Makena (formerly Hawaii's favorite nudist beach and a sunny spot now targeted for development). The resorts hug a coastline of wide, white sand beaches overlooking the islands of Lanai and Kahoolawe and are peopled with snorkelers, and whale-watchers during the winter.

Flowers, such as the queenly and expensive protea, (opposite page) are a major Maui export while the hibiscus, below, grows in wild profusion throughout Hawaii.

Lahaina, the center of Hawaii's whaling industry in the years after 1820, is a historic and trendy waterfront town in West Maui. Lahaina is liberally endowed with some of the finest restaurants on the island and is the primary harbor for the island's burgeoning water sports activities. From Lahaina Harbor sail a network of ocean-going interests: snorkeling and diving cruises, glass-bottom boat rides, windsurfing lessons, catamaran rentals, waterskiing and others. Boat charters from Maui to Molokai are fast gaining in popularity, while whale-watching cruises between November and April stir up a growing controversy. Some environmentalists are concerned that the hordes of whale-watchers are disturbing and repelling the friendly leviathans, who annually migrate to Maui waters to give birth. Meanwhile, scuba divers from around the world are discovering the fertile underwater grounds of Molokini Islet, the premier diving spot in the islands. Charters are available from Maui.

In contrast to the maritime activities of Lahaina are the petroglyphs of nearby Olowalu, where ancient stone drawings pay silent tribute to the arts and legacies of the ancients. The powers of the past are also present in the grandeur of Puu Kukui, the second rainiest spot in the Islands, and Iao Valley, the dormant crater that surrounds it. Rising like a monolith out of the isthmus connecting West and East Maui, the dramatic Iao Needle stands 2,250 feet above the valley floor.

The road to heaven — heavenly Hana — is framed by waterfalls, parks, rainbows and crenulated canyons that come crashing to the sea like curtains of green. Once you fill your car's gas tank for the three-hour, 52-mile journey from Kahului to Hana, you have made a commitment to experience one of the most sensuous drives in Hawaii.

Route 36 to Hana reportedly contains 56 bridges and more than 600 curves that switch back and forth among fern forests, eucalyptus, bamboo and waterfalls, Maui's

Facing page: Maui's courthouse building in Wailuku, top, has a sobriety not found in Lahaina (bottom), where shoppers and windows form a continual **trompe-l'oeil. Below:** *Hotels along Maui's Kaanapali coast, against a backdrop of the West Maui mountains.*

ubiquitous landmark. It leads you through state parks, over jagged black peninsulas, and above cozy little towns with names like Keanae and Nahiku, until you arrive in Hana, a settlement described by some as "the most Hawaiian place in Hawaii." Although that declaration may be disputed, what is not is Hana's singular and inescapable charm.

In fact, Hana is known more for its people and mist-covered hills than for its beaches, for this stretch of coastline is generally rugged. Just beyond Hana's small airport, the Waianapanapa State Park has cabins for rent and, along its stark, rocky perimeter, underwater lava tubes for the adventurous.

The Ka'uiki Hill is at the eastern extreme of the Hana Forest Reserve adjacent to the southeastern border of Haleakala National Park. Three valleys — Waihoi, Wailua and the well-known Kipahulu Valley with its seven pools — meander laterally through Hana like the teeth of a comb. Kipahulu is also where the

Maui's monochromes include the misty landing of an Aloha Airlines jet at the Kahului Airport and, below, the frolicking windsurfers at Hookipa Beach, considered Hawaii's most challenging windsurfing spot and one of the best in the world.

famous aviator Charles Lindbergh lived his last years and is now buried.

It helps to be prepared for the hordes of tourists who congregate at the waterfall-fed Ohe Gulch and its Seven "Sacred" Pools of Kipahulu. The pools begin in Kipahulu Valley and cascade toward the sea in tiers.

Maui's offerings run the full spectrum of activities, from hiking to "Run to the Sun" marathons to biking down the slopes of Haleakala. One particularly popular diversion on the island is a fun and spectacular bicycle cruise that takes you from the summit of chilly Haleakala down 38 miles to the Pacific, with a picnic on the way. Its organizers drive you up to Haleakala in a van, then you cruise comfortably down in a well-fitted bike and well-monitored group. Also popular are "flightseeing" helicopter tours over Maui, Molokai and Lanai; professional windsurfing at the northern coast's Hookipa Beach; and hang-gliding and hot-air ballooning over Ulupalakua.

Facing page: The circuitous Hana Highway is famous for its waterfalls, such as this particularly zesty one along the world-renowned 52-mile route. Also famed, below, are idyllic little surf spots that have been ridden by young boys for many Hawaiian centuries.

Molokai

Those who know Molokai call it "Hawaii's best-kept secret." Although word is getting out, this gem of the Hawaiian Islands is still the most pristine destination around and the one people say has the highest visitor return rate. Only 15 minutes by air and 22 miles from Oahu, Molokai is often admired from afar, over cocktails on southern Oahu or from the distant, resortish shores of West Maui.

A glance from afar, however, gives no inkling of the treasures contained on this island. It's a petite, peninsular dab of land — only 261 square miles, 38 miles long and 10 miles wide — and it's full of waterfalls, lush valleys and streams created by the three separate shield volcanoes that make up the diverse natural formations of the island. This fifth largest of the Hawaiian Islands can make your dreams of solitude come true.

Molokai went from being called the "Lonely Isle" to Hawaii's "Friendly Isle," which speaks volumes about its paradox. While its people are genuinely cordial, the mystery and isolation of its far-flung valleys suggest a primordial detachment.

For an island of its size and population — slightly more than 6,000 people — Molokai has more than its share of natural attractions and historic and archaeological sites. There are *heiau* (temples) and shrines aplenty, and a string of Hawaiian fishponds that line southern shorelines much as they have since the 15th-century. The two main towns are Maunaloa and Kaunakakai (population 2,231), where a loud whisper can be heard across the main drag and the pool hall is the center of activity. Hangouts like the Pau Hana Inn, the island's oldest pub, and the venerable Mid-Nite Inn restaurant have devout followings among local folks who gather there for foot-stomping night life or home-cooked breakfasts. What little commercial activity there is on the island can be found in Maunaloa, Kaunakakai or at the Sheraton Molokai in the Kaluakoi Resort, the island's only master-planned resort and a dominant presence along Molokai's magnificent western shoreline.

The three-mile-long Papohaku Beach, the longest

Preceding pages: *Molokai's southern shoreline borders a string of ancient fishponds such as this one, reflecting peace and tranquility with a backdrop of Lanai. Many of the nearly 100 fishponds on this stretch of Molokai have been there since the 15th Century.* **Facing page and above:** *Molokai is known for its warm and cordial people. Portraits of a father and daughter and a Kaunakakai girl, above, speak volumes of the "Friendly Isle."*

continuous stretch of white sand beach in the islands, is one of the unforgettable features of west Molokai. Above it are Kepuhi, where the Sheraton Molokai is located, and Pohakumauliuli and Kawaikui beaches. Together they form an eight-mile stretch of pristine coastline where your footprints seem like the first.

Slightly inland is the Molokai Ranch Wildlife Park, part of the 60,000-acre Molokai Ranch, the state's second largest cattle ranch. Through this park scamper giraffes, Indian black buck, sika, ibex, greater kudu and other African creatures. They provide great entertainment and photo opportunities and are perfect counterpoints to the Nature Conservancy's Kamakou Preserve, which at 4,970 feet is a delicate habitat for 250 kinds of Hawaiian plants and several rare species of Hawaiian birds, five of them endangered and two of them found only on Molokai. The Nature Conservancy, which has been given management rights to the area by the Molokai Ranch, Ltd., is attempting to protect the

The sea, sand, and treescapes of Molokai express the island's many moods and its remote, undisturbed beauty. Clouds hover over sea and shore and sand portraits, facing page, while below, driftwood breaks infinity on the road to Halawa Valley.

wildlife from pigs, goats and other disruptive factors. Of the plants in the preserve, 219 live only in Hawaii.

The last eastern outpost accessible by automobile is Halawa Valley, the only one of the island's four major north shore valleys that can be reached by car. Thirty miles from Kaunakakai, it's headed by two large waterfalls at the base of its long and narrow shape. Those who hike far enough to reach the abundant Moaula Falls will find some enjoyable swimming and the welcome peace of a valley that once sheltered Hawaiian fishermen and farmers. Ever since a devastating 1946 *tsunami* (tidal wave), Halawa has dwelled in a quiet isolation. Pelekunu Valley on the northern shoreline is even more remote, accessible by boat when the seas are calm. Some of Pelekunu's cliffs climb to 4,000 feet above sea level, and on its valley floor dense vegetation has overgrown some of the island's ancient archaeological remains.

Kalaupapa, the windswept northern peninsula, is

Facing page: A plain wooden cross in a Molokai graveyard is not yet forgotten. Below it, riders on the Molokai Mule Ride traverse the downward trek to Kalaupapa. Below: The classic neighborhood store, complete with cordial host, on the road to Halawa Valley.

perhaps the island's best-known attraction. Connected to the Kalaupapa lookout by the 1,600-foot Jack London Trail, this former Hansen's disease (leprosy) settlement sits in lonely dignity while trekkers from above maneuver the trail's dozens of switchbacks. The uncomplaining beasts of the Molokai Mule Ride are the usual way to get down there. The beauty of the village is enhanced by the immortal work of Father Damien, Joseph de Veuster, the famed martyr-priest who helped build Kalaupapa while caring for his patients there in the late 1800s.

By the time you leave Molokai, you will find that long stretches of delicious silence are more a norm than an exception.

A longtime Molokai resident, George "Peppie" Cooke, tells why he chooses to live there: "Molokai is different. It's not spoiled yet. It's no Lahaina, no Kaanapali, no Kihei, Kona, or Waikiki. This is real country, what the rest of Hawaii used to be like."

Lanai

If Molokai is considered tiny, Lanai is minute. A mere speck in the Hawaiian archipelago, Lanai is cozy, inviting and pleasantly eccentric, with a homey charm and a fiercely loyal cadre of residents.

How is it eccentric? For starters, Lanai has two service stations, one 10-room hotel, and, in one of its two cemeteries, the dead are buried chronologically.

"State law says that if you're buried within 24 hours after you die, you don't have to be embalmed," explains longtime Lanai resident Duane Black. "Most of us on Lanai don't get embalmed. We don't have too many flights in and out, and with expenses, we kind of like it that way."

As a result, there are always two open graves in the cemetery, ready for the next customer. "It's a big community thing," Black continues. "The neighbors and relatives, we all pitch in. You can die on Lanai and get yourself buried for about $150."

A look at the names in the cemetery reveals much about the island's history. Owned by Castle and Cooke Inc., which oversees its dwindling pineapple operations, the island has attracted plantation laborers since 1924, when a Boston businessman, James Dole, imported the first foreign laborers for his pineapple fields. By reading the names in the cemetery in their order of death, you can almost see the ethnic waves of immigrants as they streamed in from China, Japan, the Philippines and Portugal.

The island is more than half the size of Molokai, with nearly 140 square miles of Norfolk pine forests and ridges, moon-like rock gardens, vast acres of pineapple and deserted beaches and harbors. Like Molokai, it's part of Maui County. But unlike Molokai, it has a population of scarcely more than 2,000, all but a handful of whom live in Lanai City. Its highest point is the 3,370-foot-high Lanaihale, and its solitary hotel, the Hotel Lanai, is next to one of the two Lanai City service stations. The only airport on the island is at 1,300 feet above sea level, and the air throughout the island is crisp and cool, due partly to the towering pine forests that draw moisture to the island.

Preceding pages: Endless fields of pineapple characterize the tiny island of Lanai, but there's lots more. Facing page: Just about everyone who lives on Lanai is employed by the pineapple plantation and lives in old plantation homes, such as this happy Lanai City family. Above: The dwindling backbone of Lanai's economy, the pineapple.

Lanai has a lonely, desolate beauty all its own. Consider the primeval landscape of the Garden of the Gods misty Norfolk pine forests, and whimsical petroglyphs, facing page, and the deep, red, rich contours of its terrain, this page. Below, Molokai can be seen in the background.

"My greatest love in the world is Lanai City," says Duane Black. "The mountain air is so cool, and the people here are the friendliest in the world. Everybody waves when you drive by, and you always wave back."

Because most of the roads in the island are only marginally functional, visitors rent jeeps or four-wheel drive vehicles. A prim and prissy automobile will definitely not make it to some of the choice spots, such as the Garden of the Gods, a haunting, surrealistic landscape at the end of the Awalua Highway up north, or the Munro Trail atop Lanaihale.

On the southern shore of Lanai is Manele Bay and Hulopo'e Bay, where whales converge in the winter and spring months to frolic en masse. This is the gentlest, most inviting piece of Lanai's shoreline and a natural harbor for sailors and campers.

In eastern Lanai, at Keomuku, Shipwreck Beach and its rusting World War II wreck offshore bear testament to the notorious trade winds and rugged waters of this

coastline. It's as if the coast absorbs the buffeting for the entire island, for back in Lanai City coolness comes from the elevation and the environment is kind.

What is not so kind is the paucity of jobs, a kind of economic scourge that causes some residents to claim that Lanai exports two things — "pineapples and our kids." That statement points to a growing concern about unemployment and the predictable exodus of high school graduates. Except for a part-time veterinarian, a part-time lawyer and the town's merchants and businessfolk, this privately owned island is completely dependent on pineapple.

Still, people like Black have remained.

"When I first came here and people asked me if anything changed, I'd point to the street light or the sidewalk or the hospital. I've lived in the same house on Lanai with the same woman for 23 years. Now I say, except for the pine trees getting taller, this place doesn't change at all!"

Lanai's people: a gentle Hawaiian man, facing page, and pineapple plantation workers and managers enjoying a pau hana *— after work — party, below.*

The Big Island

Puna's a-dance in the breeze,
The hala groves of Keaau shaken:
Haena and Hopoe are swaying;
The thighs of the dancing nymph
Quiver and sway, down at Nana-huki —
A dance most sightly and pleasing,
Down by the sea Nana-huki.
— the first known reference to *hula*,
translated by **Nathaniel B. Emerson**

According to Hawaiian lore, it was on the Big Island of Hawaii, in the eastern flank called Puna, that the first *hula* was performed. When Hi'iaka, the beautiful sister of the volcano goddess Pele, sang of the swaying dance of her friend Hopoe, she made the first known mention of the sacred Hawaiian *hula*. Hopoe was a poet, the originator of the *hula*, and the one who taught Hiiaka and perhaps Pele herself to dance.

In their chants and dances today, students of the *hula* still pay tribute to these three legendary figures as well as to Laka, the patron goddess of the *hula*. *Hula* has always been dedicated to Laka with a precise protocol and such offerings as *maile leis* at *heiau* and dance platforms throughout Hawaii.

Laka presides over an ancient tradition that bears striking resemblance to South Pacific island cultures. The *hula* began as a religious, poetic and esoteric art form that was performed to influence the gods, to heal and beautify, and to celebrate life and tell stories in the form of chant, song and dance.

Thankfully, the ancient (*kahiko*) and modern (*auwana*) forms of *hula* are undergoing a dramatic resurgence today as serious students in *hula halau* (schools) undertake the arduous training required of the art. Throughout the year, *hula* competitions such as the Big Island's Merrie Monarch Festival attract the finest performers and chanters who evoke the power of Hawaii's past with their haunting, rhythmic movements set to the pulsating beat of the gourd and drum.

Having survived waves of controversy (beginning with the raised eyebrows of puritanical missionaries in

Preceding pages: A blinding majesty prevails in the snow-covered cinder cones of the Big Island's Mauna Kea, shown at an altitude of about 13,000 feet. Facing page: The Big Island's acclaimed **kumu hula,** *the late Edith Kanaka'ole, with daughters Nalani and Pua.* **Above:** *The first sign of growth in many eruption sites is the* **hapu'u,** *an endemic Hawaiian fern.*

the 1800s), the dance that originated as a spiritual expression came to encompass other, less serious levels. For one thing, it is a common form of entertainment today.

Some scholars claim that the *hula* was bound to change with the impact of Western culture and the resultant decline in the Hawaiian population and traditional life. Indeed, today you will find Chinese children, Japanese men, Portuguese, *hapa-haole* (mixed people) and every other conceivable ethnic strain among the earnest practitioners of this ancient and complex art.

A Kumu's Thoughts

Consider a *kumu's* (*hula* master's) comments:

Our school is about five generations old. That's a long tradition to keep up. I guess that's why our students project that. We stress that hula *is not only for dancing, but an art, an art style, a lifestyle. So we take into consi-*

The Big Island is vast and bountiful, with koa *forests above the Volcanoes National Park and lumberjacks who log them, facing page, and a waning sugar industry with its burning and harvesting of sugar cane, below.*

deration all the other facets of hula, *like dyeing with berries and stamping the fabric with bamboo stamps, for our costumes. We make our own skirts and collect our own* kupe'e. *That's a shell only collected on dark nights. It's probably only a week out of the month that you can collect the shell.*

We learned hula *from my grandmother, and after that, my mother took over. She died in 1979. We received most of our spiritual power from my grandmother's upbringing. She was dedicated to the* hula *so she was literally given to the gods at birth. She was taken away from her parents to live and learn on a one-to-one basis with her teacher.*

It was a more subliminal teaching then. The teacher could have been 100 miles away but he still could teach her by entering into her dream. And when she got up, she could do the dance. That's more a pure form, and that way you don't get an interpretation hang-up. Most of our dances are about 300 years old, passed down from my grandmother's kumu *and her* kumu *before that.*

I love the direction hula *is taking today. It makes for a healthy environment in* hula. *It's coming back, and it's coming back into a more traditional form. The dancers are getting more into the language too. More people are aware of the importance of the language in* hula.

It's good that hula *is used in entertainment, too. If it doesn't have that element, it's not hula. Hula has to inspire spiritually and entertain at the same time. The character of it is that there's always a transcendence. It's part of the nature of the dance. It's like the kupe'e that only comes out on dark nights: It's the character of this shell that's transcending too, because they usually bury themselves deep into the sand and only at night do they sort of transcend to earth.*

We are lucky to live and practice on the Big Island. I think it's more alive because it is the youngest of the islands. The land is more pliable to you. It's easy to feel inspired here.
— Nalani Kanaka'ole,
   kumu of the Halau Ō Kekuhi

Facing page: *Hawaii's aquaculture ventures include trout-raising in the ancient fishponds of Keaukaha, near Hilo.* **Above:** *A net fisherman from North Kohala demonstrates the skill required for what was once a major activity of the Hawaiians.*

Hula, Fire, and Ice

The Big Island of Hawaii, with its vast, expansive grandeur spanning active volcanoes, papaya, macadamia nut and coffee farms, and one of the largest cattle ranches in the United States, is still the home of *hula*, as it was when Hopoe danced in the *hala* groves of Puna. Although *kumu hula* (teachers) and their students practice diligently on all of the Hawaiian Islands, it is on the Big Island that the history of *hula* is so vitally present and the dance interwoven into daily life.

It was a natural phenomenon, for this island still vibrates with creative forces. Five large shield volcanoes form its 4,038-square-mile land mass, containing 63 percent of the total land area in the state. The island is rimmed by nearly 300 miles of rainbow-colored coastline — beaches of rugged black lava rock, green sand, black sand and white sand.

If this island, the Orchid Isle, is also called a land of

The Big Island's rich and active volcanic soil yields mist-shrouded ohia *trees, far left, the bright vandas of Kona's orchid farms, and a serene yellow cinder cone from the Kilauea Iki eruption while below, the steam banks of Kilauea's caldera paint yet another mystical landscape.*

fire and ice, it is because of the imposing presence of its summits and volcanoes. On this large and diverse island they span the extremes, from eruptions at the whim of Pele to light snowfall on Mauna Kea and Mauna Loa in the late winter months.

Mauna Kea, at 13,796 feet, is a commanding presence on the island and Hawaii's only ski slope. The "white mountain" of Mauna Kea is nearly matched in elevation by the 13,677-foot-high Mauna Loa, the "long mountain." Both are described as the highest mountain peaks on earth if measured from top to ocean base, at which point they scale the charts at 30,000 feet. Like the feisty Kilauea Crater, which at this writing has had dozens of eruptions in a two-year-long cycle, Mauna Loa is an active volcano which last erupted for 22 days in March, 1984. Both Mauna Loa and Kilauea have their summits and part of their slopes included in the Hawaii Volcanoes National Park, while the other remaining Big Island volcanoes, Hualalai (8,271 feet)

and Kohala (5,480 feet), are dormant or extinct.

Given the grand scale of its natural wonders and the sheer size of its land mass, this island requires time.

A Brave Little Town

On the eastern slopes of Mauna Kea and Mauna Loa is the town of Hilo, a brave little outpost that lives under the constant threat of lava flow or *tsunami*, the giant seismic sea waves that last decimated the coastline in 1946. With its 36,000 residents, Hilo is the most heavily populated town on the Big Island. It is also the county seat and main port for shipping the island's sugar to West Coast refining plants and is full of quaint and sometimes depressing weather.

The Lyman Mission House opens its doors to a rich glimpse of the island's past, and, in the middle of town, the Liliuokalani Gardens pay tribute to the Japanese

Facing page: One of Hilo's lasting traditions is the fish auction, where the Suisan market's array of menpachi await the highest bidder. Below, volumes of ahi, or yellowfin tuna, are unloaded at Suisan on Hilo Bay before the auction.
Below: An ethereal evening view of Mauna Kea across Hilo Bay.

with gardens, bridges and a pavilion for the traditional tea ceremony. Other favored attractions in Hilo are the Suisan Dock and fish market with its hustle and bustle that begins before daybreak, and the 80-foot-high Rainbow Falls outside of the main town.

The Hamakua Coast

The drive north from Hilo along the Hamakua Coast takes you past sugar cane fields, plantation villages and little seacoast hamlets where the ancient Hawaiians lived off the land and sea. Tiny villages with long names — Laupahoehoe, Paauilo, Honokaa — offer pockets of respite along the long Hamakua drive.

It is when you reach the northern hinterlands of the Hiilawe twin falls in majestic Waipio Valley, however, that you touch the isolation possible on this island. The falls cascade hundreds of feet into a valley that is now uninhabited, but which at one time harbored tens of

Taro, the mainstay of the ancient Hawaiians' diet, is still harvested on the Big Island today, most prominently in Waipio Valley, shown below and on the facing page.

thousands of people who grew rice, taro and lotus in an idyllic and thriving community. Horseback or jeep rides deep into the valley offer a closer look at this charmed and bewitching valley.

The Hamakua drive ends at the upcountry town of Waimea, headquarters of the 120,000-acre Parker Ranch and the closest thing to a *paniolo* — cowboy — town in Hawaii. Waimea's mist-covered highlands rise north to rugged Kohala and south to meet the northern flank of Mauna Kea, while mere minutes away is a sun-drenched coastline of turquoise waters.

Gold in Them Hills

Kawaihae, Hapuna and Puako begin what is known as the Kohala Coast, the Gold Coast of tourism in Hawaii. Hawaii's first luxury resort, the Mauna Kea Beach Hotel, is still sitting pretty at the northern end of the island's western shoreline, while other luxury

resorts crop up like mushrooms in the amber light of prosperity and upscale travel that has come to characterize this laid back and sunny area.

Some of the best snorkeling on the island exists on this coastline, where petroglyphs, old lava flows, desert flora and ancient fishponds meld into a landscape that crashes into a brilliant, reef-rich sea. Even with the presence of the Kohala Coast's new resort developments, you can almost hear the drumbeats and the chants of ancient fishermen as they appealed to the gods for a bountiful harvest from the sea.

At the eastern point called Keahole, where the island's second and smaller airport is located, the mood and ambience changes as the Kona Coast begins. This is a stretch of ancient *heiau*, big game fishing, seafood restaurants and suntanned tourists.

Kona is the sunniest place on the island, an older, more casual counterpart to the posh new Kohala Coast. Kailua-Kona, its proper name, refers to the upland

Waimea, also called Kamuela, and the vast Parker Ranch acreage make up paniolo *country on the Big Island, where branding, rodeos, and smiling Hawaiian cowboys continue the western tradition.*

neighborhoods, formerly the domain of coffee farms, and the shoreline tourist areas. The 8,000-foot summit of Hualalai is visible along this stretch of West Hawaii.

If someone asks you about "Kona Gold," he's referring to the *pakalolo* that grows abundantly in the hills of West Hawaii. In some circles, Kona Gold has a higher recognition factor than looming Mauna Kea or the annual Kona Billfish Tournament that really put the town on the map. In fact, a recent year's "Green Harvest" police confiscation sweep put the Big Island's marijuana haul at nearly 83 tons, at an estimated value of more than $33 million.

While Kona is studded with hotels, it's also only a few miles away from some of the Big Island's more significant historical sites, such as Kealakekua, the site of Captain Cook's sudden death in 1779, and Honaunau's City of Refuge, formerly a sacred place of refuge where fugitives were harbored by holy men. The City of Refuge is a national park with a reconstructed

Portraits of Big Island teenagers depict a mixed bag of many ethnic origins, as seen in the eighth-grade graduating class of the Hawaii Preparatory Academy, facing page, and other young people, shown below.

village, canoes, sky-high coconut trees and venerable lava rock walls built many years ago.

Green Sands and a Red Hill

The long southern route from Kona to the volcano area meanders through old and new lava flows and meets Ka Lae, or South Point, the southernmost point in the U.S. and the first landfall made by Hawaii's Polynesian settlers. South Point looms majestically at the end of an 11-mile road through ranch land, and it borders a beach colored green by the finely ground crystals of olivine, remnants of a collapsed cinder cone.

It is an austere and windswept coastline and should leave you ready for the varied spectacle of the Hawaii Volcanoes National Park, 208,000 acres of rare plants and birds, cinder cones, steam vents, volcanic lava tubes, piquant *ohelo* berries, and a full agenda of smells, colors and folklore unlike any in the world.

The elaborately painted St. Benedict's Church, built in 1912, depicts the strong Christian influence in Hawaii (facing page), while below, an ancient heiau *in the Puukohola Heiau National Historic Site stands as a mighty testament to ancient Hawaiian worship. Only Hawaiians practicing their native religion are allowed beyond this point.*

Volanic eruptions cause a rush on hotel reservations and helicopter tours as they attract viewers from all over the world at only a moment's notice. Residents and visitors in the know leave offerings of *ti*, gin and brandy at the rim of Kilauea Crater, said to be the home of Pele. Nearby, the trails, lookouts and the Volcano Art Center are eminently worth exploring, and the national park has spartan cabins for rent if you want to linger longer.

The Volcanoes National Park also contains an 18-mile trail to the summit of Mauna Loa, where the Red Hill cabin holds lonely vigil over a surrealistic terrain. A long uphill hike and occasionally arctic Volcanic eruptions cause a rush on hotel reservations from trekking up this mountain, but those who do say the spectre of pink dawn and opalescent ash are well worth the strenuous climb.

Eruptions from the summits of Volcano naturally course downward, as in 1977 when the village of

Kalapana was threatened by a lava flow that stopped within a half-mile of the town, or in 1960 when crumbly *a'a* inched through cane fields and swallowed the town of Kapoho. Residents of the Royal Gardens subdivision have had to evacuate fairly regularly in Kilauea's most recent eruptive phase, when houses were flattened and damaged. The phenomenon makes for a kind of frontier, pioneer spirit among those who dwell on the flanks of a volcano, and it changes the complexion of the earth as well.

The landscape-altering process of vulcanism is evident in the black sand beaches of Kaimu and Punaluu on the southeast shoreline of the island, where lava pulverized into sand creates long stretches of exotic black beach highlighted with luminous olivine. In the hills near Pahoa, steam-emitting cracks attract local residents for a sauna above the sea; at least one steam vent is known to have ladders and sitting places for its users. It's a very cool hot spot indeed.

Facing page: *The Big Island's features include warrior petroglyphs along the Mauna Lani Hotel's historic trail, above, and Kilauea's ongoing eruptions, such as this one in 1985.* **Below:** *Surfers after a full and rainy day on the rocky coast near Hilo.*

Kauai's many-splendored beauty includes the Spouting Horn in Poipu, above, and the rugged and awesome Na Pali coast on the island's north side, facing page, where hidden valleys long ago sheltered taro farms and lost tribes. This area is only accessible to hardy hikers, helicopters and boats.

Kauai

On the far northern end of Kauai, near Ke'e Beach at Haena, the remnants of the *hula* platform of a former Kauai chieftain, Lohiau, still stand like a timeless sentinel. This three-tiered *heiau* is where offerings to Laka were and still are made.

Hawaiian legend tells of the journey of Pele's wandering spirit to a *hula* festival at that spot, where she and the handsome young chieftain fell in love. Ancient chants and *mele* are full of references to the long and treacherous journey endured by Pele's sister, Hi'iaka, ordered to Haena to bring Lohiau back home to her sister on the Big Island.

The Lohiau *heiau* in Haena recalls the earliest days of the *hula* and is adjacent to the trailhead that leads into Kalalau Valley on the island's awesome Na Pali Coast. This is an area of immense and unfathomable power, imbued with the mystical forces that the Hawaiians believed shaped the Islands.

Kauai and its neighbor, the privately owned Niihau, were the only two islands not conquered by Kamehameha by warfare but united instead by agreement, years after the other Hawaiian Islands were conquered in the 1795 Battle of Nuuanu. It is also the oldest, and, some believe, the most rugged of the islands, accorded a special place in the hearts of ancient and contemporary Hawaiians.

Only 26 minutes by plane from Honolulu, the Garden Island is 548.7 square miles in size and was formed from a single shield volcano. The fourth largest of the Hawaiian Islands, it is encircled by 90 miles of beach — some estimates put it at 43 beaches — girding the island. It is an island of backwoods charm and a kind of innocence, and on its north shore are what many contend are the most magnificent sea cliffs in the world as we know it.

The Na Pali Coast, viewed in awe from land, sea and air, is the stellar result of nature's chiseling through the forces of erosion. An annual average of 450 inches of rain falls upon the wettest spot on earth, Mount Waialeale, then courses into the Alakai Swamp and down the precipitous gorges of the Na Pali Coast,

Facing page: *Hollywood producers spend millions trying to reproduce Kauai's tropical beauty on the screen, and no wonder. This island's jungle-clad mystique beckons relentlessly.* **Above:** *Another kind of beauty: the people. An entertainer on a Wailua River boat ride displays her sense of* aloha.

painting this coastline in deep, dark greens and purples. Hollywood producers spend millions venturing into the Kalalau Valley and attempting to capture its beauty on celluloid, while stalwart hikers who attempt its 11.5-mile trail find themselves rewarded with waterfalls, mountain pools, deserted beaches, sea caves and abandoned terraces where taro once grew.

The Hanakapiai Loop Trail, which leads from the Kalalau Trail to the famous Hanakapiai Beach, is the shortest and most manageable segment into the valley. It will lead you along fluted canyon walls that crash to the sea while plume-tailed tropical birds soar overhead.

Also available to hikers is the Alakai Swamp Trail from the other side of the mountain at the other end of the highway, in Kokee. Although it's also in the northern sector of the island, Kokee is a couple of hours from Haena. Between the two, along the coastal highway route, are the inhabited areas of the island.

The Alakai Swamp, at 10 square miles the largest

Facing page: The view from a helicopter at more than 5,000 feet high inside Waialeale Crater, the wettest spot on earth, shows waterfalls streaming like tears down a face. **Below:** *On the other side of the crater is Ke'e Beach at Haena, on the island's north shore, not far from a historic* **hula** *temple.*

and most exotic in Hawaii, is a primeval forest of bogs, thickets and rich natural habitats for some of Hawaii's rarest birds and plants. Endangered species of honey-creepers with bright feathers and curved beaks dart gaily from branch to branch of trees that may be dwarfed due to the peculiar conditions of Alakai.

Also in Kokee is the 4,000-foot-high Kalalau Lookout — breathtaking — and a series of trails that meander gloriously through the Kokee State Park. The Kokee Museum and the Kokee Lodge, a restaurant, provide information and respite while several miles down the road the fabled Waimea Canyon offers another rapturous view: deep, ribboned gorges etched in yellows, sienna, greens and purples, and resounding with the bleating of the wild goats which live there.

Moving down from the upcountry Kauai, you may come upon Polihale Beach Park, one of the widest expanses of beach to be found. If conditions permit, the privately owned island of Niihau will be visible on the

Facing page: Bamboo fisherwomen in Hanapepe Valley take a break. Below them, ancient driftwood against stone paints a portrait in blue and green. Below: Waimea Canyon, an ever-changing palette of rusts, greens and purples, is home for colonies of goats and heaven for its viewers.

horizon. Polihale is one of several stunning west coast beaches that are accessible but not overcrowded — but because of its riptide, it should be approached with an experienced swimmer's caution.

On the way to Lihue, on the main highway, you will pass Waimea, where Captain Cook first landed in 1778, and where the Menehune Ditch is located. The ditch and its counterpart in Lihue, the Menehune Fishpond, are believed to be the remnants of the boundless skills and labors of Hawaii's legendary *menehune*, a leprechaun-like race said to have performed gargantuan deeds only at night. The two sites are a singular example of esoteric stonework, unlike any other in ancient or modern Hawaii.

Poipu, one of three resort areas on Kauai — the others are Princeville and Wailua-Kapaa — dominates the south shore with its rash of hotels, restaurants and surfing and swimming spots. Not far from the popular Pacific Tropical Botanical Gardens in Lawai, Poipu

offers the driest, sunniest conditions on Kauai. Wind-surfing is burgeoning here as sailboard-wielding surfers from the other islands discover the joys of wave-riding in the clear waters off Poipu. Excellent snorkeling and diving conditions prevail as well.

Neighboring Koloa, an old plantation town undergoing extensive renovation, provides a heady dose of local flavor in this otherwise touristy area. And the real coup is the gateway to Koloa, Knudsen Gap — a stretch of road shaded by a canopy of towering eucalyptus trees that hold golden light in the late afternoon as if crowning you with its halo.

It is on the eastern stretch, from Lihue to Kapaa, that the majority of Kauai residents live. In Wailua, where the Wailua and Opaekaa falls feed into the river, riverboat activities and beaches such as Lydgate offer a wide range of activities, from kayaking or water-skiing up the river, to boating up to the Fern Grotto, to safe swimming for kids at the sheltered Lydgate beach.

Lihue, with its population of 4,000, and Kapaa, with some 500 people more, make up the island's major centers of activity. Night life is limited to a few hotel night clubs and isolated discos, but no one on the island really expects the Ginza. Kauai has respectable restaurants but it's a daytime island with a natural environment as its strongest suit.

About an hour and many bridges from Lihue, you come upon Kilauea, an old plantation town known for its lighthouse, fresh corn and the Kong Lung Store, very chic and quite nostalgic. Kilauea is also the gateway to the island's North Shore, where wild guava, mountain apples and streams and rivers with fresh *o'opu* fish and black night herons are part of the real-life canvas. From Hanalei Bay to Lumahai, and on to the wet and dry caves of Haena, the north coast of Kauai is a series of dazzling bays, turns and *hala*-lined beaches around every bend of its curious one-lane and narrow wooden bridges.

The valleys and arches of the island include the taro fields of Hanalei Valley, facing page, a Japanese arch in Kalaheo's Kukuiolono Park, and below, the view from inside the Na Pali Coast's "blue cave," accessible by boat and Zodiac inflatable craft.

110

Hanalei is also a rich piece of history, a place where ancient taro fields are still green, wet and neatly patchworked, and where efforts to rebuild an old rice mill pay homage to the island's immigrants. With its current influx of *nouveau-riche* vacationers, Hanalei has remained refreshingly unpretentious. The sprawling but well-planned Princeville Resort development, with its own tiny airport and fairytale views on all sides, was wise to make Hanalei its home.

Hanalei. The word means "crescent bay," and the reason for this name becomes obvious when you drive along Hanalei Bay and marvel at this broad anchorage and its beautiful curving sands bordered by ironwoods. Transpacific yachtsmen often linger in this spectacular anchorage to psych themselves up for even more remote Pacific adventuring. Hang out under a big Hanalei moon for a while, and you'll soon understand why Hollywood chose this area as its filming site for the movie "South Pacific."

Facing page: *Princeville's vacation condominiums, above, and Koloa town's old storefronts portray light and the birth of night* Below: *Happy faces from an evening at Aunty Margaret's Bar in Hanapepe.* Following pages: *A study in amber and mauve, from a sunset view of Niihau, taken from the town of Kekaha.*

Local Style

Local style is:

— keeping your shoes outside the door
— wearing surf shorts instead of bermuda shorts
— the "shaka" sign
— keeping your bathing suit in the trunk of your car for quick dips
— owning only one jacket
— sleeping in *puka* (hole-y) t-shirts
— wearing shoes without socks
— going to cockfights
— playing the *ukulele* by the beach at sunset
— plate lunch with "two scoop rice"
— telling tourists that pineapples grow on trees
— saying "brah"
— *sashimi* and *sushi* by the seashore
— crack seed and mango ice cream
— *saimin* with homemade noodles
— being late (Hawaiian time, a.k.a. "Polynesian paralysis")
— "rock fever"
— double rainbows
— bodysurfing with one fin
— sex wax
— 40-cent *manapua* from the lunchwagon
— Puna papayas
— *opakapaka* diablo
— Oahu open markets
— campaigning on street corners
— *huli-huli* chicken and chili-and-rice fundraising *luaus*
— *shoyu* on formica tables

The "shaka" sign is real local style, as shown by State Sen. Neil Abercrombie, with friend, facing page, and a cordial cane truck driver from Koloa, above. Learn the shaka sign and its spirit and you're in Hawaii.

The above list is a crash course in orienting your eyes, ears and taste buds to the inimitable nuances of being in Hawaii. "Talking local" here means knowing your *mahimahi* from your *malihini* and *ewa* from *whatevah*. It also means knowing that *brah* is a euphemism for "you" and not a twin-peaked accoutrement for a part of the anatomy.

But no one expects the visitor to absorb all the idiosyncrasies of Hawaii, so don't worry. Besides, local style changes some of the time. That means that today's neon shoelaces and clove cigarettes, black vinyl purses and green lipstick may be gone in a flash, supplanted by the fickle winds of The New Trend.

With Hawaii's truly local touches, it's usually simpler. We don't have pink mohawks and Cyndi Lauper hair. Instead, we have some things that do last, like keeping shampoo in the glove compartment to shower at the beach, or starlight concerts at the Waikiki Shell, or dinner at the harbor-side Tasty Broiler, where they reimburse you for your parking meter deposits, or *shoyu* on formica tables in Hawaiian restaurants, or Matsumoto's *shave ice* with azuki beans, or people-watching at the Ala Moana Center ... but after a few months here, you'll get da idea, brah.

Facing page: Local style is streetside lobbying, campaigning, and protesting, day-glo vests on newspaper boys, and pretty, freshly dusted dumplings from a mochi *store in Moiliili.* **Below:** *Only in Hawaii would you find* shoyu *on every table and such novel delectables as hula pie.*

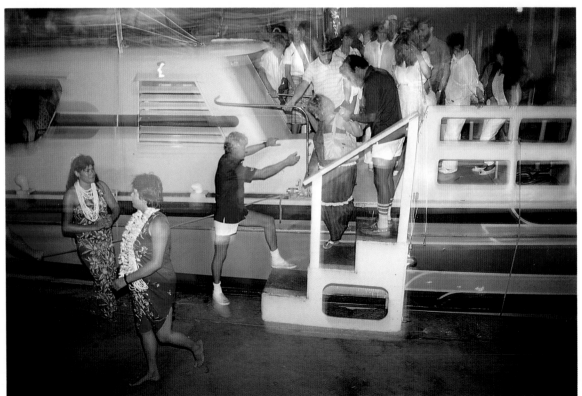

Tourism

Tourism is a double-edged sword and the nerve center of the state's economy. While it brings in 4.8 million visitors a year who pump about $4.5 billion into Hawaii's economy, Hawaii's number-one industry is a constant threat to some local residents who fear it affects the quality of life in the islands. But in an economy in which agriculture is waning rapidly and high-tech is struggling to be born, tourism is impossible to ignore, whatever your opinion.

Figures from the state and the Hawaii Visitors Bureau show that visitors to Hawaii in a recent year created $477 million in tax revenues. Jobs related to the tourist industry totaled 164,500. On any given day in 1984, an average of 118,000 tourists from the U.S. mainland and the East, primarily Japan, were vacationing in Hawaii.

What do they do? According to the *State of Hawaii Data Book*, there are seven national parks in the state, "74 state parks, 626 county parks, 57 golf courses, 259 public tennis courts, 2,023 small-boat moorings, 1,600 recognized surfing sites, and 24.4 miles of safe, sandy, accessible beach."

In addition, recreational attractions that recorded more than a million visitors last year include the Honolulu Zoo, the Hawaii Volcanoes National Park, the Wailua River State Park, the U.S.S. Arizona Memorial and the National Memorial Cemetery of the Pacific (Punchbowl).

The Hawaii State Legislature in 1985 appropriated $5.2 million for the promotion of tourism by the Hawaii Visitors Bureau. In addition, regional promotional organizations such as Destination Molokai, the Waikiki Beach Operators Association, the Kaanapali Beach Operators Association and the Poipu Beach Operators Association are busily and successfully attracting new waves of visitors to their respective areas. Maui, meanwhile, is leading the pack in Neighbor Island visitor traffic with its two million annual visitors.

The Big Island's Kohala Coast and its opulent luxury resorts represent what many feel is the future of Hawaii tourism: "upscale" travel. When the Hyatt Waikoloa

Facing page: *Whether they're strolling through Waikiki's International Market Place or jumping off a Lahaina cruise boat, tourists always have fun in Hawaii.* **Above:** *An unforgettable feature of the 48-year-old Kodak Hula Show is the contemporary Hawaiian man representing the classic Hawaiian warrior.*

adds its presence to the coastline inhabited by the Mauna Kea Beach Hotel and the Mauna Lani Bay resort, the Kohala Coast will be even more firmly established as a tourist center to be reckoned with.

The Military

A local activist group called the Protect Kahoolawe Ohana has been battling the military for some time, claiming that its use of that tiny, uninhabited island as a field for bombing practice is an abuse to both the land and its spirit.

The military owns Kahoolawe, but because Kahoolawe contains archaeological sites and is part of the *aina* (land) that is Hawaii, Hawaiian activists continue to protest. It is a peacetime battle that takes on symbolic proportions in a finite island state in which the military presence claims nearly six and a half percent of the total land mass. According to some

Facing page: A grim reminder of lives lost in war, at Oahu's National Memorial Cemetery of the Pacific at Punchbowl, and below it, workers at the Pacific Missile Range in Kauai's Barking Sands.
Below: *A U.S. Army vessel stops at Kawaihae Harbor on the Big Island for military exercises.*

reports, 260,000 acres of the 4.1 million acres of land on all the islands of Hawaii belong to or are used by the five branches of the U.S. military.

Indeed, the armed forces are among the top owners and users of Hawaii's land. Most of the federal land is in wildlife, park and military use; on Oahu, where 26 percent of the land is owned by the armed forces, military use predominates.

What this means in terms of population is this: 12 percent of Hawaii's 1,039,000 population consists of military personnel and their dependents. They spend money in Hawaii, pay taxes and are indirectly wooed by a state attempting to attract more federal dollars into its coffers. Cutbacks of civilian workers at the Pearl Harbor Naval Shipyard have caused much alarm as legislators and union officials gird themselves for swelling unemployment figures. But the crisis, and a concurrent decline in Hawaii's agricultural industries, have put pressure on government leaders to lend

THE SOLEMN PRIDE
THAT MUST BE YOURS
✗ ✗ TO HAVE LAID ✗ ✗
SO COSTLY A SACRIFICE
UPON THE ALTAR
OF FREEDOM

Facing page: *The Canada/France observatory is only one of the world's most powerful telescopes that sit atop Mauna Kea.* **Above:** *Soon this snow-covered site on the Big Island's most prominent landmark will contain the world's most powerful telescope.*

greater support to the development of high-tech industries in Hawaii.

Reaching for Stars

High atop the 13,796-foot-high Mauna Kea, like mushrooms rising out of craters on the moon, telescopes from different countries are probing the mysteries of the universe. Mauna Kea, the Big Island's towering presence, contains the world's biggest and most powerful collection of astronomical observatories, a cluster of the world's best, with cumulative capital costs of $53 million so far.

This is impressive to science, industry and the state, and to muses who might ponder the implications of looking back 12 billion years in time.

One of the new telescopes planned will be the largest and most powerful in the world. The California Institute of Technology will build a telescope with the amazing capability of looking back to nearly three-quarters of the life in the universe. This nearly imponderable thought means that science, as represented atop Hawaii's own Mauna Kea, is inching closer and closer to what astronomers say is the time when the galaxies were formed. When this ultimate, $70-million telescope is complete in 1991, it will be the ninth on the star-reaching mountain, and so powerful it will be capable of detecting the light of a 15-watt bulb on the moon.

Such capabilities offer a new look at Hawaii's place in the world. Few other locations offer the possibilities of geothermal, ocean thermal, volcanic, astronomical and geological exploration as does the frontier of Hawaii. Here, where ancient Hawaiians prayed to the gods and harvested their food from the sea...where gods and goddesses ended their travels from the mystical land of Kahiki...where boundless activity in the earth's inner core gives new life to the study of creation...where a new island is forming inch by inch thousands of feet under water...and where the outer reaches of science come to the slopes of Mauna Kea...here is Hawaii — sustaining, still, her people.

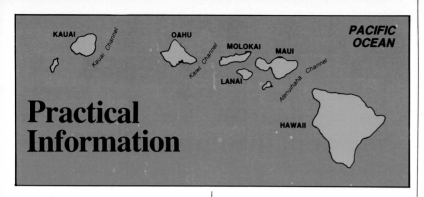

Practical Information

Hawaii. On the Neighbor Islands there is no public transi
rented car, hotel shuttles,
or tour buses are the norm.

Visitor Information

The Hawaii Visitors Bureau
(Honolulu)
2270 Kalakaua Ave.
Honolulu, HI 96815
Phone: 923-1811

The Hawaii Visitors Bureau
(Kauai)
Suite 207, Lihue Plaza Bldg
3016 Umi St.
Lihue, Kauai, HI 96766
Phone: 245-3971

The Hawaii Visitors Bureau
(Hawaii)
75-5719 W. Alii Drive
Kailua-Kona, HI 96740
Phone: 329-7787

The Hawaii Visitors Bureau
(Hawaii)
Suite 104, Hilo Plaza
180 Kinoole St.
Hilo, HI 96720
Phone: 961-5797

Destination Promotion
Associations:

Maui:

Maui Visitors Bureau
172 Alamaha
Kahului, Maui, HI 96732
Phone: 871-8691

Wailea Destination Assn.
P. O. Box 3440
Honolulu, HI 96813
Phone: 525-6640

Kaanapali Beach Operators
Assn.
2530 Kekaa Drive
Lahaina, Maui, HI 96761
Phone: 661-3271

Climate

What you've heard is true: In Hawaii there are basically two seasons, April to November, when it's 73°F to 88°F, and the rest of the year, when it's damper and cooler, at 65°F to 83°F. Except in Kona weather conditions,when southerly winds cause mugginess, the days and nights are usually cooled with tradewinds. This means you can travel light to Hawaii. Unless you plan to hike Haleakala or stay in Kokee, a light jacket or sweater will do, with warm-weather, casual clothes for daytime.

Arrival

You will arrive at either the Honolulu International Airport, the Kahului Airport on Maui, the Lihue Airport on Kauai or the Big Island's Hilo Airport. The three Neighbor Island airports receive only a limited number of direct mainland flights, so most of Hawaii's arrivals still land in Honolulu.

Citicorp at the Honolulu International Airport provides currency exchange, and there are Deak Perera offices throughout Waikiki and downtown. American Express offices are at the Hilton Hawaiian Village, the Hyatt Regency Waikiki and the Waikikian.

Three major inter-island airlines — Aloha, Hawaiian, and Mid-Pacific — provide daily air service to the Neighbor Islands. There are also several small commuter airlines providing service to some airports not served by the large carriers. These include: Royal Hawaiian Air Service; Air Molokai; Reeves Air and Princeville Airways. You may also go to Lanai by boat from Maui with the Ocean Activities Center — Phone: 879-4485.

Tipping

Tips are not included in restaurant tabs or in taxi fees. Customary gratuities are 15 or 20 percent.

Transportation

Oahu's TheBus service costs 60 cents. Transportation to Waikiki from the Honolulu International Airport is offered by Sida Taxi, Gray Line Hawaii, a limousine service, and the Waikiki Express. Major car rental companies have counters at all the major airports in

Kauai:

Poipu Beach Resort Assn.
P. O. Box 788
Koloa, Kauai, HI 96756
Phone: 742-7444

North Shore Assn.
Paul Palmer, President
c/o Bank of Hawaii
Princeville, Kauai, HI 96714
Phone: 8256-6551

Hawaii:

Kona Visitors Assn.
8-7000 Alii Drive
Kailua-Kona, HI 96740
Phone: 322-3866

Kohala Coast Assn.
P. O. Box 4959
Kawaihae, HI 96743
Phone: 885-6677

Molokai:

Destination Molokai Assn.
P. O. Box 1067
Kaunakaki, Molokai, HI 96748
Phone: 567-6118

Oahu

Shopping

Ward Centre
Ward Warehouse
Ala Moana Center
Royal Hawaiian Center
Aloha Stadium Swap Meet,
Saturdays and Sundays at the
Aloha Stadium
People's Open Markets (Island
Produce). Phone: 523-4808

Museums

Iolani Palace, downtown,
Phone: 536-2474
Bishop Museum, Kalihi,
Phone: 847-1443

Special Outings

Kodak Hula Show, Waikiki
Shell . Phone: 941-1611

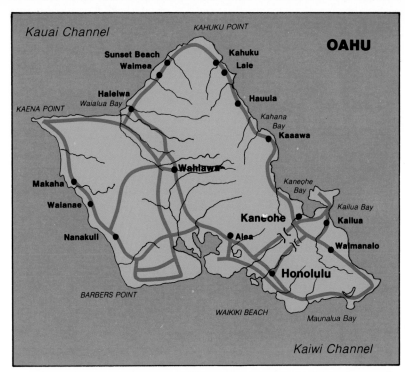

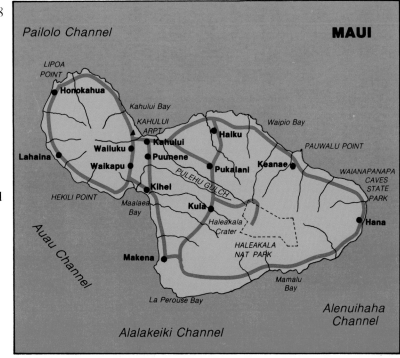

Lyon Aboretum, Manoa.
Phone: 988-3177
Moanalua Valley Hike,
Phone: 826-6551
Waimea Falls Park.
Phone: 638-8511
Glider rides: Honolulu Soaring
Club. Phone: 623-6711

Maui

Special Outings

Cruiser Bob's Rent-a-Bike,
biking down from Haleakala.
Phone: 667-7717
Iao Needle
Ulupalakua

Molokai

Special Outings

Molokai Mule Ride.
Phone: 552-2662
Wildlife Safari. Phone 553-5115
Mountain Adventure.
Phone: 553-5936
Royal Helicopters.
Phone: 567-6733;
839-0644 (Oahu)

Lanai

Jeep and Car Rentals

Oshiro Service Station
P. O. Box 516
Lanai, HI 96763
Phone: 565-6952

Lanai City Service
P. O. Box N
Lanai, HI 96763
Phone: 565-6780

Big Island

Parks

Volcanoes National Park
Hawaii National Park, HI 96718
Phone: 967-7311

Island of Hawaii (state parks)
P. O. Box 936

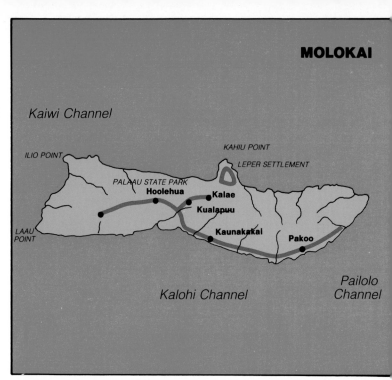

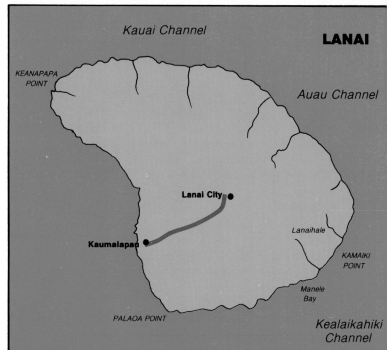

Hilo, HI 96720
Phone: 961-7200

Kauai

Special Outings

Wailua River boat ride, Smith's
Boat Ride or Waialeale Boat
Tours
Lady Ann Cruises, Nawiliwili.
Phone: 245-8538
Na Pali Zodiac, Hanalei.
Phone: 826-9371
Island Adventure, Nawiliwili.
Phone: 826-9381
Grove Farm Homestead
Museum, Lihue.
Phone: 245-3202
Pacific Tropical Botanical
Gardens, Lawai.
Phone: 332-8131
Horseback Riding
Highgates Ranch, Kapaa.
Phone: 822-3182
Princeville Activities Centre,
Princeville. Phone: 826-9691
Kauai Canoe Expeditions.
Phone: 245-5122

Caveat

Never leave valuables in your
car or trunk. Tourists are
primary prey for vandals.
Use a sunscreen. The tropical
sun can be ruthless.
Don't walk barefoot on a coral
reef. It may contain spiny
creatures that could hurt you.
Avoid swimming at North Shore
beaches in the winter.

Cruises

American Hawaii Cruises
550 Kearny St.
San Francisco, CA 94108
Phone: (415) 3929400

Seven-day inter-island cruises
aboard luxury liners,
S.S. Constitution and

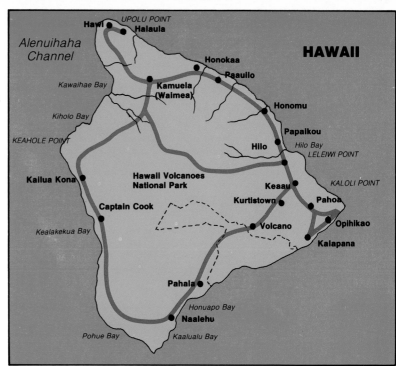

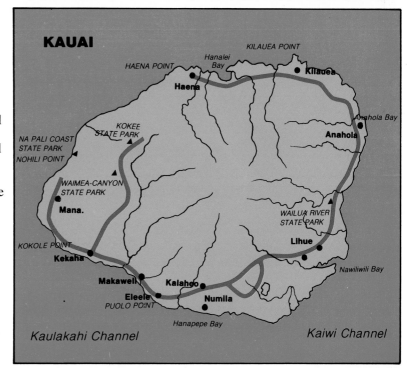

Photography by
Frank Salmoiraghi
Text by
Jocelyn Fujii
Printed in Singapore
January 1986
Publisher's number: 266

Additional photos are by
Valerie Kim (dustjacket
portraits), Ed Robinson
(page 38) and Warren
Bolster (page 40)